Andrew Brown is a barrister called to the Bar of England and Wales in 2014 who specialises in insolvency and commercial law with a particular emphasis on fiduciary duty claims against directors, reviewable transactions, and corporate restructurings. Prior to his career as a barrister, Andrew earned a Masters and a Doctorate in Ancient Greek History from the University of Oxford where he also lectured on various ancient topics.

A Practical Guide to Void Dispositions and Validation Orders

A Practical Guide to Void Dispositions and Validation Orders

Andrew Brown

Barrister, Lincoln's Inn

BA, BA, MPhil, DPhil (Oxon)

Law Brief Publishing

Published 2025 by Law Brief Publishing, an imprint of Law Brief Publishing Ltd
30 The Parks
Minehead
Somerset
TA24 8BT

www.lawbriefpublishing.com

Paperback: 978-1-916698-90-1

To Andrew Kopkin –

A barrister, educator, and mentor.

Thank you for first setting my feet

on the path to being a barrister.

PREFACE

As readily apparent to all those who practice in the field, void dispositions are a constant thread of insolvency work. They are the natural by-product of compulsory court ordered insolvencies, and range from miniscule sums to significant transactions requiring court proceedings. They can be innocent mistakes, and they can be the subject of bad faith attempts to strip assets from an insolvent entity. They can be simple transactions, or they can be complex dispositions involving questions of banking law. In whatever shape they come, they can be deceptively tricky, and occasionally maddeningly straight-forward.

This book aims to provide the barest of practical introductions to this subject to those practising in the field of insolvency law, as well as those who are merely dipping their toe in the subject from other specialisms for a single set of instructions. The goal of this work is to provide a practical overview of the nature of the void disposition, how it might be identified so that monies can be reclaimed for an insolvent estate, how those facing such claims might defend or validate the transaction, and the basic procedure of doing so. I have no intention of delving into the theoretical legal principles underpinning how void dispositions operate or the position of the recipient post insolvency (eg. as a constructive trustee or otherwise), and merely make reference to these principles where applicable but leave the deep legal learning and hypotheticals about future developments to more learned and larger secondary sources. Instead, I focus on the practical points that I have seen in my own experience, and the questions that immediately arise when faced with a brief. I have tried to make this text as approachable as possible in my own inimitable writing style viewed through the lens of my experience as an insolvency litigator. Thanks to my background of having operated in cases ranging from the most mundane of small claims in the county courts to significant matters worth billions of pounds, I have seen the breadth of what might crop up, and have attempted to distil that learning.

As an important note, the law in this text is up to date as of 15 May 2025 when it was finalised, but the field of insolvency law is a moveable feast, and every day brings new case-law and updates. If you are reading this at a distance from the second quarter of 2025, then be aware there might have been significant updates not contained in this book.

Thanks to all those who have discussed the nature of void dispositions with me, and special thanks to my colleagues who are always willing to provide sounding boards for discussions of tricky legal problems or matters of procedure, and in particular: Jonathan Edwards as the font of all legal knowledge (insolvency or otherwise), my colleagues and members of the area of chambers known as '*the Gulag*' for their irreverence, Jeremy Cousins KC for leading me on my first significant insolvency trial concerning void dispositions (amongst other matters), and all the members of Radcliffe Chambers who have made it the most pleasant and supportive work environment I have ever known.

Most of all, I offer my most grateful of thanks to my wife, Rosalie Barrett, for her continued and long-suffering support for my oft time-intensive career, for putting up with my screams of frustration late at night when I relive mistakes made in court, and for keeping my feet on the ground when I relive my successes. Finally, to my children: Jamie, Annabelle, and Eddie for the joy that they bring to life.

Andrew Brown
May 2025

CONTENTS

CHAPTER ONE

INTRODUCTION

Dispositions made void pursuant to the Insolvency Act 1986 are amongst the most common and mundane of insolvency related claims that lawyers and insolvency practitioners are likely to see. Nearly any person, corporate or real, who holds and exchanges assets and is made insolvent by order of the court is likely to have a number of dispositions of property that are subsequently rendered void by operation of statute. Depending on the length of the period between presentation of a petition and an insolvency order, then these might be significant and number in the thousands. This book aims to provide a basic introduction to these most regular of insolvency claims, and provide the practitioner with practical guidance for how to identify and recover void dispositions and/or defend against attempts to do so by an office-holder.

As with all insolvency related claims, it is important to remember the fundamental and defining purpose of insolvency law: to preserve, gather, and distribute the assets of an insolvency estate on an equal and ratable basis amongst the unsecured creditors proving within that estate. While the interests of secured and preferential creditors do intrude into the administration of insolvent estates from their lofty heights, this fundamental principle of equal treatment amongst the unsecured is what is commonly referred to in insolvency as the '*pari passu*' principle, and underpins the treatment of most matters, ie. that all unsecured creditors should be treated equally without preference, and that the interests of the body of creditors as a whole is the guiding interest for insolvency proceedings. This guiding principle is highly relevant within the context of void disposition where their nature is to avoid the preferential treatment of a particular creditor who has received benefit in the 'relevant time' at the expenses of the greater body of creditors, and also provides one of the gateways for the granting of validation orders to avoid the effects of automatic voiding, eg. that a particular disposition benefits the greater body of creditors as a whole rather than the individual creditor involved. Any practitioner involved in an investigation or prosecution of a void disposition claim should keep this fundamental principle of insolvency law in the back of their head.

As shall be examined in this book, the basic nature of the void disposition is straight-forward as it is merely the automatic statutory consequence of an order of the court for the winding-up of a company or an individual's personal bankruptcy, and as a result the legal basis of a claim is simple. However, the devil is always in the details, and a wise practitioner must be careful of what might be laying the tall grass of an otherwise apparently simple claim. This book seeks to simplify the practical realities of what is a void disposition, what are its exceptions, how a recipient party might defend against a claim for repayment, and how a potential insolvency person or a recipient might seek the court's blessing to validate a specific payment. What is set out in this text is a set of examples and principles drawn not only from case-law, but also focused by my own experience at the coalface.

Throughout this text there will be copious references to the Insolvency Act 1986 and the associated Insolvency Rules 2016, which are the statute and statutory instrument that governs the insolvency regime in England and Wales. For brevity, where I refer to the Insolvency Act 1986 it shall be noted as 'IA 1986,' and where I refer to the Insolvency Rules 2016 it shall be noted as 'IR 2016.' Likewise, when I make reference to the Practice Direction on Insolvency Proceedings I shall reference it as the 'PDIP,' and the Civil Procedure Rules (where appropriate) as the 'CPR.' All other statutes will be spelled out in full, as with any other statutory instruments. I shall endeavour to use neutral citation where possible for case-law, but when one is not available (such as cases from the pre-neutral citation watershed), then I shall use the appropriate law report. I make limited to no reference to other secondary sources in the market, but encourage those with deeper questions to turn to those sources if they cannot find an answer in my text or are interested in deeper theory.

As a final note, this book focusing on the law in England and Wales, which is where I am called as a barrister. There are some differences in the insolvency regime between England and Wales and Scotland, such as the Scottish statutory causes of action for 'gratuitous alienation' and 'unfair preferences' under ss.242 & 243 IA 1986 as opposed to the English and Welsh ss.238 and 239 for transactions at an undervalue and preferences. I am not an expert in the law of Scotland, although I understand that s.127 and s.284 IA 1986 apply equally in that jurisdiction. I do not include in this text any specific Scottish case-law, and caution any of those reading this in Scotland to consider whether local case-law might lead to a different application.

CHAPTER TWO

THE NATURE OF VOID DISPOSITIONS

This chapter focuses on the basic concept of what is a '*void disposition*,' and seeks to break down the subject into the constituent elements of such a disposition: what is meant by void, in what insolvency context does it occur, when does it occur, what is meant by a '*disposition*,' and what exceptions might exist to the definition of '*disposition*.'

The concept of the void disposition is contained within two sections of the IA 1986: s.127 in relation to corporate insolvency, and s.284 in relation to personal bankruptcy. The texts of these sections not only contain the legal effect of a compulsory order on certain dispositions, but also the elastic clauses giving rise to validation orders (see Chapter Four, below), and the statutory defence in personal bankruptcy in favour of Equity's Darling (see Chapter Three, below).

S.127 IA 1986 governs corporate compulsory winding-up:

> ***127Avoidance of property dispositions, etc.***
>
> *(1) In a winding up by the court, any disposition of the company's property, and any transfer of shares, or alteration in the status of the company's members, made after the commencement of the winding up is, unless the court otherwise orders, void.*
>
> *(2) This section has no effect in respect of anything done by an administrator of a company while a winding-up petition is suspended under paragraph 40 of Schedule B1.*

(3) This section has no effect in respect of anything done during a moratorium under Part A1, or during a period mentioned in section 5(4)(a) following the end of a moratorium, where the winding-up order was made on a petition presented before the moratorium begins, unless the petition was presented under section 367 of the Financial Services and Markets Act 2000 on the ground mentioned in section 367(3)(b) of that Act.

S.284 IA 1986 governs personal bankruptcy:

284 Restrictions on dispositions of property.

(1) Where a person is made bankrupt, any disposition of property made by that person in the period to which this section applies is void except to the extent that it is or was made with the consent of the court, or is or was subsequently ratified by the court.

(2) Subsection (1) applies to a payment (whether in cash or otherwise) as it applies to a disposition of property and, accordingly, where any payment is void by virtue of that subsection, the person paid shall hold the sum paid for the bankrupt as part of his estate.

(3) This section applies to the period beginning with the day of the making of the bankruptcy application or (as the case may be) the presentation of the bankruptcy petition and ending with the vesting, under Chapter IV of this Part, of the bankrupt's estate in a trustee.

(4) The preceding provisions of this section do not give a remedy against any person—

> *(a) in respect of any property or payment which he received before the commencement of the bankruptcy in good faith, for value and without notice that the bankruptcy*

application had been made or (as the case may be) that the bankruptcy petition had been presented, or

(b) in respect of any interest in property which derives from an interest in respect of which there is, by virtue of this subsection, no remedy.

(5) Where after the commencement of his bankruptcy the bankrupt has incurred a debt to a banker or other person by reason of the making of a payment which is void under this section, that debt is deemed for the purposes of any of this Group of Parts to have been incurred before the commencement of the bankruptcy unless—

(a) that banker or person had notice of the bankruptcy before the debt was incurred, or

(b) it is not reasonably practicable for the amount of the payment to be recovered from the person to whom it was made.

(6) A disposition of property is void under this section notwithstanding that the property is not or, as the case may be, would not be comprised in the bankrupt's estate; but nothing in this section affects any disposition made by a person of property held by him on trust for any other person.

There is an understandable practice amongst many to conflate the company and personal insolvency regimes under ss.127 and 284 as so analogous so as to be mirror images, but this is dangerous (*Re Flint* [1993] Ch. 319). As set out below, the majority of the learning on these regimes can be read across both sections, but there are distinct differences between them that can sink the case of the unwary, and I shall seek to set out those differences below where relevant.

What is the 'relevant time' for a void disposition

When we speak of void dispositions we speak of insolvent estates that have been created by compulsion of court order, but there are some anomalies with the associated regimes of voluntary liquidation, administration, the company moratorium under Part A1, and the insolvent estates of deceased persons. The relevant time in which void dispositions arise and the special circumstances in relation to other insolvency regimes are set out below.

Compulsory Corporate Winding-Up

S.127(1) defines the 'relevant time' for void dispositions as being '*after the commencement of winding-up*.' To the uninitiated, this would appear to be a reference to the date of the winding-up order itself, but that would be a mistake. The rules of commencement are as follows:

- S.129(1) IA 1986 defines the '*commencement of winding*-up' as being the presentation of winding-up petition. Where a 'new' creditor has 'substituted' their debt into the petition such that it is amended, then the winding-up date remains the initial presentation of the petition (*Re Western Welsh International Buildings Ltd* [1985] 1 BCC 99, 296), which can have profoundly negative effects if the initial petitioner's debt has been paid off from company assets (see below on this eventuality).

- Tricky questions can arise as to when exactly a winding-up petition is 'presented.' Recent authority indicates that a petition is not formally presented until a petitioner complies with all conditions set by statute including the payment of the Official Receiver's deposit (*Re A Company* [2024] EWCA Civ 1436). This can raise problems if there is a gap between filing of the papers and payment, and in particular if a petitioner seeks to rely on a cheque. There is Australian authority that a disposition made on the same day as the presentation of a petition is not caught by the avoidance provision in that statutory regime (*Re Skypac Aviation Pty Ltd* [2019] NWSC 291), but it remains to be seen if such an approach will be followed in England & Wales.

- As an example: If a petition was issued on 1 January 2025, but the petition was adjourned multiple times until a final court order winding-up the company occurs on 1 January 2026, then despite the order coming a year later the actual '*commencement of winding-up*' would be deemed to occur on 1 January 2025, and any transaction falling in the interim would automatically be rendered void.

- The effect of the time-lag between presentation of a petition and a winding-up order can be mitigated by notice of the petition on the company's bank. Most banks monitor the winding-up list, and will freeze company bank accounts upon notice of a petition in order to preserve the company's assets. The effect of this is that advertisement or notice of the petition can be deadly for a company as it effectively paralyses its ability to trade barring validation orders, and such a situation is the source of many applications for validation orders and injunctions to restrain advertisement of a petition. A similar situation is not present in personal bankruptcy as advertisement of the petition is not required, and banks are unlikely to freeze a personal account that would otherwise be needed for the basic necessities of life for the debtor and their family.

As an important distinction, in the context of a corporate insolvency, the void disposition regime under s.127 only applies to those companies which have been wound-up by order of the Court, and not those which exist solely within the voluntary regimes. S.127 specifically notes that it applies '*in a winding-up by the court.*' It is a common practice that companies will enter creditors voluntary liquidation ('CVL') after presentation of a winding-up petition. In such instances, payments made between the presentation of the petition and the resolution to enter voluntary liquidation will not be void under s.127, which is a small loophole in the regime, although they would be potentially caught by other avoidance provisions such as ss.238 or 239 IA 1986.

One final legacy note exists as a holdover from the dark days of the Covid-19 pandemic: those petitions presented in the period between 27 April 2020 and 30 September 2021 fall outside the general statutory rules. Pursuant to Schedule 10 paragraphs 8,9, and 21 of the Corporate Insolvency and Governance Act 2020, the '*commencement of winding-up*' is the date of the winding-up order itself. This was a special measure introduced to deal with the extraordinary consequences of the pandemic and the various temporary amendments to the prosecution of petitions in that period. As commencement is upon the winding-up, there are no void dispositions to speak of (other than post-order dispositions where the directors have no power to dispose of company assets), so this need not concern us beyond this basic point.

Personal Bankruptcy

The eagle-eyed amongst this book's readers will have noted that the statutory regime for personal bankruptcy does not mirror word-for-word that of compulsory liquidation of a company, but the effects are very similar.

- S.284(3) defines the 'relevant time' for a void disposition as falling between the presentation of the bankruptcy petition and the vesting of the estate in the trustee in bankruptcy.

- In the case of an individual who is made bankruptcy on a petition presented by a creditor resulting in a bankruptcy order, then the vesting occurs at the timing of the bankruptcy order (s.306 IA 1986). The Official Receiver is appointed as trustee in bankruptcy as a matter of statute (s.291A(1) IA 1986), unless a petition is presented by a supervisor of an individual voluntary arrangement who seeks to be appointed trustee.

- The bankruptcy regime requires a statutory demand to have been served prior to the presentation of a winding-up petition, but this demand and its presentation or service is irrelevant for void dispositions – it is only the issuing of the bankruptcy petition which is relevant.

- As with company petitions, it is suggested that the statutory requirements of presenting the petition must be complete before it can 'commence' winding-up (see by analogy, *Re A Company* [2024] EWCA Civ 1436, which would include the payment of the deposit, etc). Likewise, where a substitution of creditor takes place within an existing petition, the original presentation of the petition remains the starting point for the relevant time and not the amendment.

The period between the presentation of a petition and the bankruptcy order in personal bankruptcy can be much longer than in corporate winding-up as courts are likely to give adjournments to individuals who put forward credible payment plans, and due to the overburdened court system the listing time for bankruptcy petitions in the county courts often result in long delays between hearings. As individual bank accounts are not 'frozen' by the banks in the same fashion as corporate accounts, this can lead to significant numbers of dispositions that are void ranging from small daily sundry purchases to large financial transactions. It is likely for this reason that the specific defence in favour of third parties receiving dispositions in good faith for value and without knowledge of the petition exists, as otherwise there would be an impossibly large amount of void disposition claims clogging the court system.

Personal bankruptcy has a specific quirk absent from compulsory liquidation of companies whereby an individual person might apply for their own bankruptcy. In such instances, the 'relevant time' is not in reference to a bankruptcy petition, but to the presentation of the bankruptcy application (s.284(3)) and the subsequent adjudication of bankruptcy. In practice this can often happen in a very short period of a few days (or shorter), although the impact can be significant if an individual makes themselves bankruptcy while in litigation so that they lose title to funds they have disposed to meet an unless order with the result that they are in breach of the unless order and suffer its consequences (*Re Razeem* [2024] EWHC 2368 (Ch)).

The insolvent estate of a deceased individual

Where an individual dies, and is subsequently deemed to be insolvent, then the applicable law under the IA 1986 is modified by the Administration of Insolvent Estates of Deceased Persons Order 1986 ('the 1986 Order').

Where a deceased's estate is unable to meet its debts, then a creditor of a deceased individual can present a petition for an insolvency administration order. Pursuant to Paragraph 12 of Schedule 1 of the 1986 Order, the date of the petition's presentation is deemed to be the same date as the deceased's death. As a result, payments made between the deceased's death and the making of the insolvent estate administration order will be rendered void (*Re Vos (Deceased)* [2006] BPIR 348), although the statutory defence of Equity's Darling will remain.

For validation orders concerning the insolvent estates (see Chapter Four, below), the Court will seek balance the interests of creditors with those of beneficiaries (*Wegwood v Hosein* [2024] EWHC 1836 (Ch)).

<u>What about other insolvency regimes?</u>

Rules as to Creditor Voluntary Liquidations of companies

As noted above, a CVL which follows presentation of a winding-up petition will prevent s.127 IA 1986 applying, and a CVL which is resolved in a vacuum will likewise not incur any issues of void dispositions.

The one exception to this rule is that pursuant to s.88 IA 1986 the transfer of shares or alteration of the membership of a company after the commencement of a voluntary liquidation is void – unless sanctioned by the liquidator. Commencement of a voluntary liquidation occurs upon the resolution to place the company into liquidation per s.86 IA 1986 (also *Re Norditrack (UK) Ltd* [2000] 1 WLR 434).

The transfer of shares and alternation of the membership of a company is precluded to prevent shareholders who might hold shares that are not paid-up from escaping liability. Pursuant to s.74(1) & (2)(d) IA 1986, any member of a company is liable to contribute to the insolvency up to the value equivaled of any unpaid shares held in the company. In practice, many shares are valued at '£1,' and unless the shareholding is large then the sum payable is nominal, but in some instances the value per share can be much higher or the number of shares can be a significant so as to incur a large liability. This restriction on disposition of shareholding is also contained in s.127(1) IA 1986 in relation to compulsory winding-up.

Finally, CVLs can move to compulsory liquidation, and in such instances s.129(1) deems that the '*commencement of winding-up*' occurred with the resolution to voluntarily wind-up the company, but it also states that unless the court directs otherwise as a result of fraud or mistake the proceedings of the voluntary winding-up (including any dispositions of the company's property) are deemed to be valid. This exists to protect the liquidator of the CVL who might have made interim distributions to creditors in the intervening period or paid expenses such as legal fees in regard to administering the insolvent estate.

Rules as to administrations of companies

As with CVLs, companies might enter the alternative insolvency regime of an administration rather than be wound-up by the Court. This procedure is temporary in its nature, ostensibly a 'rescue' vehicle, and limited in length at first to 12-months, but it can be extended by an unlimited number of further 12-month periods. While it is ostensibly part of the rescue culture of modern insolvency law, the reality of most administrations is they are an alternative form of liquidating a company, and many administrations move into voluntary or compulsory liquidation after some time.

- A winding-up petition will be 'suspended' where an administration order is made after its presentation (paragraph 40(1)(b) Schedule B1 1986 Act), and if the company subsequently enters compulsory liquidation upon that suspended petition following conclusion of the administration, then nothing done by the administrator(s) of the company will be void pursuant to s.127(2), which is analogous to the position for CVLs that move into compulsory liquidation. This will not affect any dispositions made between the presentation of the petition and its suspension by the administration (*Harlow v Creative Staging Ltd* [2014] EWHC 2787 (Ch)).

- If a petition has been presented prior to an administration application, then the petition will be adjourned to the hearing of the administration application. If the administration application is dismissed, then the Court will consider whether to make a winding-up order upon the petition, and if it does so then the winding-up will commence in the normal fashion.

- Conversely, upon an administration application where no petition is presented, the court retains the power to make a compulsory winding-up order if it thinks it appropriate (paragraph 13(1)(e) Schedule B1 1986 Act), and if it does so, then pursuant to s.129(1A) 1986 Act the winding-up is deemed to commence on the making of the order. In such circumstances there will not be any void dispositions to consider as no relevant time exists.

Rules as to Moratoriums under Part A1 for companies

While rarely seen, the effect of the statutory moratorium under Part A1 1986 Act is an exception to the normal timing of commencement of winding-up. Where a petition has been presented prior to a moratorium under Part A1 commencing, then s.127 does not apply to anything done during the moratorium, or in the period prescribed by s.5(4)(a) 1986 Act where a company voluntary arrangement ('CVA') is sought following conclusion of a moratorium. A CVA is in theory supposed to be a regular exit approach from a moratorium, but in practice very few moratoriums have existed so this point has not appeared in any reported cases.

As an exception to the moratorium special rules, where a petition was presented by the Financial Conduct Authority pursuant to s.367 Financial Services and Markets Act 2000 in relation to an insurance undertaking or reinsurance undertaking on a just and equitable ground then the moratorium rules will not apply.

Provisional Liquidation of companies

Provisional liquidation is the process whereby a 'provisional' liquidator is put into place by an order of the Court where a winding-up petition is pending. This is done in circumstances where there is a risk of dissipation of assets by the company or its directors and/or that company records might be destroyed. The provisional liquidator is appointed to 'hold the ring' pending the resolution to the petition, and while a later winding-up is likely there remains the possibility that the petition will ultimately be dismissed. If a winding-up order is made subsequently, then it will apply in the normal fashion with relation back to the petition, although the imposition of a provisional liquidator will likely mean that no dispositions have occurred in the meantime.

What is meant by 'Void'

There is no special art or meaning to the definition of '*void*' under ss.127 and 284 IA 1986, and the word has its natural meaning. The effect of the sections is to render void any disposition of the insolvent's assets so that it has no legal basis. This is to be contrasted with 'voidable,' which is a concept whereby a transaction can be attacked and 'reversed' by order of the court or the election of a contractual right. In the real world, creditors often respond to being told that payments they have received some time before an insolvency order are 'void' by conflating this with 'voidable,' and refusing to recognise their lack of title to the proceeds of the disposition unless or until a court makes an order. In reality, once a winding-up or bankruptcy order has been made, then any disposition is automatically avoided without any other action needing to be taken, and the only consequential action requiring court orders are remedies for restitution compelling a third-party recipient to repay or return the asset disposed to them.

The result is that unless the disposition falls into one of the exceptions discussed below, then it is simply taken to have no legal basis so that the asset (or its value) must be returned to the insolvent estate.

What is a 'disposition;'

As with the definition of '*void*,' there is no specific definition for '*disposition*' within the words of the IA 1986, the IR, or the PDIP, and its meaning has been the subject of case-law defining its scope.

- A '*disposition*' has most recently been held to be the reduction in value of a right of the debtor in favour of an accrual in value in favour to another person (usually a creditor) (*Re Officeserve Technologies Ltd (in liq)* [2018] EWHC 2168 (Ch)). An important point is that the debtor who makes the '*disposition*' has a beneficial interest in the asset disposed so that it effects the overall value of the insolvent estate (*Re Branston & Gothard Ltd* [1999] BPIR 466). Thus, where property is held on trust by a company and that company transfers legal title to the property to a third-party, then there is no disposition as the insolvent estate never had a beneficial interest and suffered no loss.

- As an example, a disposition by a receiver appointed pursuant to an equitable charge given prior to the presentation of a petition will not be avoided. This is because the company's equity was already charged in favour of the third-party and the receiver merely realised the property in favour of the third-party's existing rights over the equity (*Sowman v David Samuel Trust ltd* [1978] 1 WLR 22).

- Both ss.127 and 284 IA 1986 concern the '*disposition of property*,' and the broad meaning of disposition should be read in consideration with the equally broad definition of '*property*' in s.436 IA 186. This defines '*property*' as being:

  > *"money, goods, things in action, land and every description of property wherever situated and also obligations and every description of interest, whether present or future or vested or contingent, arising out of, or incidental to, property"*

- As a result, disposition do not merely concern the transfer of cash or money held in a bank account, although these are the most likely types of void dispositions due to the nature of life, but also catch the disposition of land, choses in action, physical assets such as artwork, and so forth.

- Finally, bankruptcy and insolvency in England and Wales applies to all of an insolvent's property throughout the world. As a result, the effect of ss.127 and 284 IA 1986 are said to have ex-territorial effect to that they apply to assets located outside of England and Wales (see *Akers v Samba Financial Group* [2017] UKSC 6, which concerned the disposition of shares in the Kingdom of Saudi Arabia). The effect is that if a company or person is made insolvent in this jurisdiction, but has a bank account in the United States, then dispositions from that bank account to third parties are caught by the sections and avoided. The practical difficulty in such circumstances will be recognition of the insolvency in any foreign jurisdiction able to enforce rights, which can be easy or difficult depending on the jurisdiction and any treaties governing the recognition of insolvency practices.

The easiest way to identify what dispositions are caught, or not caught, is to consider basic examples:

- The most obvious of dispositions caught by ss.127 and 284 IA 1986 are payments of money from the insolvent estate to a third-party recipient, and any payment after presentation of the petition will be void unless validated or subject to the special rules set out below. A regular example would be the post-petition payment of a creditor's debt that was incurred pre-petition (*Re Liverpool Civil Service Association* [1874] 9 Ch. Appl. 511). Such payments are not only dispositions, but they are analogous to a preference in that a creditor is receiving payment while other creditors are not. However, as a potential exception payments to creditors incurred after presentation of the petition in the normal course of business might give rise to a good ground for a validation order (see more below, Chapter Four).

- Likewise, the gratuitous gifting of an asset to a third-party recipient would constitute a disposition, such as the gifting of a piece of art to a bankrupt's spouse, and would be analogous to transactions at an undervalue.

- The surrender of a lease held by an insolvent individual, release of a contractual right, or release of a charge over property owned by third parties would likewise constitute a disposition as the third-party would accrue value by being free of the encumbrance, and the insolvent estate would suffer detriment by losing the value of the same (*Akers v Samba Financial Group* [2017] UKSC 6). Likewise, an agreement not to sue on a debt is equivalent to a release of that debt and is a void disposition (*Officeserve Technologies Ltd (in liq)* [2017] EWHC 1920 (Ch)).

- However, there must be an actual transfer of value, so that the collection of a book debt owed *to* the insolvent estate is not a disposition despite the extinguishing of the chose in action giving rise to the right to collect. Rather, the chose in action's value is merely converted into the money now in the person's bank account.

- However, the bare assignment of a chose in action from the insolvent individual to a third-party would also constitute a disposition as '*things in action*' are clearly included within the definition of '*property*.'

<u>Special Rules as to particular dispositions:</u>

Payments into and out of the insolvent's bank accounts

The lay person often views a bank account as containing 'their money' held in a specific account which is accessible to them whenever they choose, but that does not reflect the legal reality of how bank accounts work. When an account is in credit, the bank owes money to the account holder, the chose in action of which can be converted into cash being given by way of withdrawal or via payment to a third-party at the behest of the account holder. Conversely, when an account is overdrawn, the account holder owes money to the bank so that 'payment into' the overdrawn account reduces the account holder's debt to the bank. This relationship has created vexing problems for how ss.127 and 284 IA 1986 operate in relation to payments into and out of bank accounts after the presentation of a petition.

There are four basic categories of bank payments which must be considered:

- When an insolvent pays money into a bank account that is in credit: there is no void disposition. While technically the insolvent is transferring ownership of the funds paid to the bank, it is replaced with a chose in action equivalent to the same sum (*Re Barn Crown Ltd* [2995] 1 WLR 147). There is technically a disposition in such an instance, but there is no detriment to the insolvent person's estate unless the bank becomes insolvent so that it cannot repay the chose in action when called upon later by the office-holder. The bank will need to account for the value of the funds 'held' in the account to the office-holder as an asset in the insolvent estate.

- When an insolvent pays money into a bank account that is overdrawn: this would constitute a void disposition. The reasoning is that in such circumstances the insolvent person owes money to the bank as a loan (the overdraft), which is reduced by payment into the overdrawn account swelling the assets of the bank as a creditor while reducing those of the insolvent (*Re Gray's Inn Construction Co Ltd* [1980 1 ALL ER 814). There might be a validating ground where the bank can show that a reduction in the overdraft was a requirement by the bank to allow the insolvent to continue to use the account and therefore benefit the overall body of creditors. The bank will be liable in such circumstances to repay these sums, but if an overdraft remains at the date of the insolvency order then it will likely be able to make use of the insolvency set-off as a defence (see more below, Chapter Three).

- When an insolvent pays money out of a bank account that is in credit: this would constitute a void disposition in favour of the third-party who receives the payment. The reasoning is that the insolvent reduces their chose in action against the bank in favour of accrual in value to the third-party recipient. While this is a void disposition, no action exists against the bank as it acts merely as the agent of the insolvent (*Bank of Ireland v Hollicourt (contracts) Ltd* [2000] EWCA Civ 263).

- When an insolvent pays money out of an overdrawn bank account: this would constitute a void disposition – although not without some controversy. It has been held that payments out of an overdrawn account can constitute void dispositions (*Re Gray's Inn Construction Co Ltd* [1980] 1 All ER 814). There has been much ink spilled on this topic which considers the analysis in *Gray's Inn* was wrong as it was a point not argued but merely conceded by counsel, and it has elsewhere been held that the increase in an overdraft up to its limit does not constitute a disposition (*Coutts & Co v Stock* [2000] 1 WLR 906). However, the current law appears to be that such circumstances would lead to a void disposition in favour of the third-party recipient who has increased their asset position. Any claim would be against the third-party recipient and not the bank.

In summary of the above, with the possible exception of an instance where an insolvent repaid the entirety of its overdraft with the bank during the relevant period, there is unlikely to be a good cause of action against a bank. In some instances banks might be liable for breaches of their *Quincecare* duty of care where they allow payments to be made that are an obvious fraud (*Philipp v Barclays Bank UK plc* [2023] UKSC 25), such as when the bank is aware of the potential or likely insolvency of a company and a director actions significant payments out of the company's account in favour of third-parties (*Re*

Singularis Holdings Ltd [2019] UKSC 50). However, this is an entirely different type of claim from a void disposition.

Payment of cheques after the petition

Cheques are not traditional payments, and can create confusion between whether a disposition occurs when a cheque is 'drawn' or when it is 'presented' for payment.

- By way of example, a cheque may be made out on a Monday, a bankruptcy petition presented on the Tuesday, and the cheque presented for payment by the third-party to the bank on the Wednesday. This raises the natural question of whether the payment under the cheque is void or not as did the disposition occur with the drawing of the cheque and thereby promising payment upon presentation, or when the payment was actually actioned upon presentation of the cheque to the bank.

- There are a number of conflicting authorities on the nature of void dispositions and cheques, but most recently in the Insolvency and Companies Court it has been held that it is the payment of the money upon presentation of the cheque which will constitute a disposition rather than the drawing of the cheque itself (*Re Changtel Solutions UK Ltd (in liq)* [2022] EWHC 694 (Ch)). However, the judge also noted in *obiter* remarks that the drafting of the cheque post-petition would have constituted a void disposition.

Trust assets and the special circumstances of Akers v Samba

As noted above, it is only assets in which an insolvent has a beneficial interest that might form the basis of a void disposition, so in instances where an insolvent holds property on trust for a third-party, then a disposition of the legal title of the property by the insolvent trustee is not a disposition within the meaning of ss.127 or 284 IA 1986. This is explicitly set out in s.284(6) IA 1986, which excludes trust property from its ambit.

A more difficult question arises when the insolvent has a beneficial interest in assets held on trust by a third-party who disposes of the asset in such a fashion that the insolvent's interest is overreached or destroyed by Equity's Darling.

- In *Akers v Samba Financial Group* [2017] UKSC 6, the Supreme Court had to consider an instance where an insolvent company had an interest in shares which were held on trust by trustees. The trustees transferred legal title to the shares to a third-party.

- In such circumstances, only the legal title, and not the beneficial title, transferred, and the insolvent company had no property in the legal title. As a result of the transfer of the legal title for value and without notice of the company's beneficial interest the purchasing third-party took the shares free of any trust as Equity's Darling.

- No disposition of the company's beneficial interest occurred, so s.127 IA 1986 was not engaged despite its beneficial interest then being overridden. It did likely have a breach of trust claim against the trustee.

Completion of property purchases

A relation point to the trust law set out above is the aspect of the law of property in England and Wales concerning the distinction between the exchange of contracts for sale of real property and the completion of sale.

- Upon the exchange of contracts for the unconditional sale of land, the vendor of the land holds it on constructive trust for the purchaser whereby the vendor retains no equitable interest in the property, although they do have a lien over the purchase monies. The subsequent completion of purchase unifies the legal and equitable title in the purchaser extinguishing the constructive trust. Where the exchange of contracts are for a sale conditional upon a subsequent event occurring, then the position is likely to be different.

- As a result, the competition of a purchase of land *after* the presentation of a petition, but where the contracts had bene exchange *prior* to the presentation of the petition will not constitute a void disposition within ss.127 or 284 IA 1986 as the purchaser will have already acquired beneficial title to the property under the purchaser's constructive trust (*Re French's Wine Bar Ltd* [1987] 3 BCC 173). Therefore, on completion only the legal title of the property passes from the insolvent to the third-party and not the equitable value of the property.

Shares in the insolvency company

As with the case of CVLs, explored above, s.127 IA 1986 specifically includes the transfer of shares post-presentation of a petition as being void. The logic is the same as set out above, that the mischief sought to be avoided is the disposition of unpaid shares from members who would otherwise have to pay for their unpaid shares in any subsequent liquidation.

Matrimonial dispositions and court orders

There is no statutory exception for dispositions made pursuant to orders of the court, so that an individual who is under compulsion to pay sums to an ex-spouse under the Matrimonial Causes Act 1973 will still have made a disposition that is avoided by s.284 IA 1986 by complying with the order (*Re Flint* [1993] Ch 319; *Warwick v Trustee in bankruptcy of Yarwood* [2010] EWHC 2272 (Ch)). As a general rule, and with some exceptions, insolvency law trumps family law in most instances (*Woodley v Woodley (No2)* [1994] 1 WLR 1167). However, this general approach might be met with some resistance in the family courts, and insolvency practitioners appearing on behalf of trustees in bankruptcy are advised to come to any hearing in the family courts armed with strong case-law on their behalf as there is likely to be significant push-back from the former spouses as litigants.

It is likely that an order garnishing of an insolvent person's money by way of third-party debt order would also fall to be a void disposition despite the insolvent individual having no agency in making the disposition. The effect is that during the relevant time prior to the insolvency order a third-party is taking assets in preference to all other creditors, which runs directly contrary to the fundamental rule of insolvency as set out in the Introduction to this text.

Acts that occur due the effluxion of time or without benefit to a third-party

A disposition requires some agency to constitute a proper act, so that something that occurs merely by the effluxion of time will not constitute a '*disposition.*' An example is the expiration of a leasehold by expiration of its term without renewal (*Re Officeserve Technologies Ltd (in liq)* [2018] EWHC 2168 (Ch)). This is merely the inaction of the insolvent in not seeking an extension of the leasehold, so that no '*disposition*' occurs. However, in such circumstances directors of a company who let a potentially valuable leasehold asset expire might face subsequent fiduciary duty claims for causing loss to the company, and especially in the context of their knowledge of the company's likely insolvency and/or any connection they might have to the freeholder who can then grant a new leasehold to third parties.

As an allied point, the deliberate destruction or waste of assets without any corresponding value accruing to a third-party would not constitute a '*disposition.*' For instance, a lumber company which set its timber on fire would not be conducting a disposition, but any director who directed such a fire be lit would likely be the subject of a misfeasance claim.

Realisation by a third-party holder of security over the insolvent's assets

The realisation of security by a third-party over the property of the insolvent person will not constitute a disposition. The sale by a mortgagee of a property where the mortgage has fallen into arrears is not a 'disposition' where the conveyance is by the mortgagee or a receiver appointed by them on behalf of the insolvent person (*Sowman v David Samuel Trust Ltd* [1978] 1 All ER 616). Similarly, the vesting of the insolvent's property in a secured creditor who has an after-acquired property clause within the security instrument is not a disposition by the company. Finally, and as noted above, the realisation of security over an equitable interest such as the appointment of receivers by way of an equitable charge will not constitute a void disposition.

Special exceptions in personal bankruptcy

The definition of a bankrupt's estate under s.283(2) IA 1986 specifically excludes from the vesting in their trustee in bankruptcy basic items such as tools of trade, vehicles needed for employment, clothing, bedding, and items necessary for the basic domestic needs. The purpose of that exclusion is to mitigate the potentially harsh repercussions of bankruptcy vesting by allowing a bankrupt to continue to trade and earn money in order to provide for themselves or their family. No such protections exist under s.284 IA 1986 for dispositions, and s.284(6) IA 1986 specifically includes within its ambit all of the property otherwise excluded from the bankrupt's estate. This would appear to create a strange situation whereby a trustee in bankruptcy could claim a void disposition for the gratuitous gifting of a bankrupt carpenter's woodworking tools and require return of those goods, but would then be faced with the curious situation of whether the trustee could then claim these returned tools were part of the bankruptcy estate or whether they revested solely in the bankrupt as their tools of trade. I do not know of any cases in which this has occurred.

Certain Financial Transactions

Certain financial transactions have statutory exceptions outside the ambit of ss.127 and 284 IA 1986. In practice these types of dispositions are rare, and I have not had to deal with any of them in my experience. If the company being wound-up is heavily integrated into financial markets, then there is a greater chance that these will arise.

- Pursuant to ss.163(4) and 175(3)-(5) Companies Act 1989, market contracts or other disposition of property pursuant to such a contract, the provision of margin in relation to market contracts, or a market charge fall outside the ambit of s.127 IA 1986 and are not avoided. Similar provisions apply to s.284 IA 1986 in personal bankruptcy.

- Pursuant to the Financial Markets and Insolvency (Settlement Finality) Regulations 1999 (SI 1999/2979) reg.16(1), s.127 does not apply where property of a company becomes subject to a collateral security charge. Similarly, reg.19(3) disapplies s.284 IA 1986 in instances of personal bankruptcy.

- Pursuant to the Financial Collateral Arrangements (No2) Regulations 2003 (SI 2003/3226) reg. 10(1), s.127 does not apply to the insolvency of a collateral-taker or collateral-provider under a financial collateral arrangement.

Payment of the petition debt

A common occurrence when a person faces a petition, either corporate or personal, is that they seek to pay the petition debt from their own funds. This can be dangerous for the creditor unless a validation order is obtained.

- Winding-up and bankruptcy petitions are class-remedies that are taken to have been brought by one creditor on behalf of *all* of the insolvent individual's creditors. The result is that any creditor who has a valid and partitionable debt may apply to be substituted into the petition so as to replace the original petitioner. In the case of company winding-up petitions, any creditor with a debt of £750 can substitute into the petition. In the case of a personal bankruptcy petition, the creditor must have a debt of £5,000 and have presented a statutory demand prior to issuing of the petition.

- If substituted, a creditor can prosecute the petition for their own unpaid debt, which might result in an insolvency order being made. In such circumstances the date of '*commencement of winding-up*' is the presentation of the original unamended petition (*Re Western Welsh International Buildings Ltd* [1985] 1 BCC 99, 296).

- The unfortunate result for the original petitioning creditor is that if they had their debt paid from the funds of the insolvent individual, then that settlement payment is void under ss.127 or 284 so that they need to repay those funds despite the petition debt having been settled and the original petitioner no longer prosecuting it (eg. *Harlow v Creative Staging Ltd* [2014] EWHC 2787 (Ch)).

- As a result, the petitioner and/or insolvent person will need to either: (1) apply for a validation order (see below, Chapter Four) in respect to the settlement payment, which might be difficult to impossible if there are significant other creditors outstanding so that the test for validation will not be met, or (2) have a third-party pay the debt who then seeks an indemnity from the debtor when and if the petition is dismissed. In company cases, the second category often takes the form of a director or shareholder offering to pay or secure the debt from personal funds and assets. In personal bankruptcy cases the spouse or other family member of a debtor will often seek to pay the debt on their behalf.

- These approaches mitigate the risk of a settlement payment being avoided, although can put the third-party in the position of becoming a creditor of the insolvent if the winding-up / bankruptcy order is subsequently made on another debt. This indemnity from the debtor to the third-party who has paid the petition debt is not a '*disposition*' within the context of an insolvency (*Re Hood (A debtor)* [2020] EWHC 3232 (Ch)).

- Legal representatives for the petitioner must be careful to advise their clients not to use the insolvency process as a debt collecting tool, and must be careful when advising on settlement that the settlement funds are either validated or come from a third-party.

This rule is also important in the context of bankruptcy where a defence to a petition is where the debtor has offered to secure or compound a debt. A creditor need not accept payment from a debtor where it has knowledge of other creditors who might substitute into the petition (*Smith v Ian Simpson & Co* [2001] CH 239).

Legal fees

There is no special rule protecting the right of a debtor facing a petition to pay legal fees in their own defence. As such, if a debtor pays fees to legal advisors and is subsequently made insolvent, then those legal advisors will need to repay those sums as they are rendered void.

- As a result, legal advisors typically require third parties to pay their fees on account prior to the hearing of any petitions and on behalf of the debtor, such as directors/shareholders of a company or spouses of an individual. This is a point that inexperienced legal practitioners acting on behalf of debtors often overlook, and in particular young counsel who have not dealt with insolvency matters regularly.

- Validation orders in favour of legal fees can be obtained where appropriate (see Chapter Four, below), and the court has previously opined that it is more likely to grant a validation order in respect to legal fees for a real person facing bankruptcy than a company (*Andrew v Kingsway Leasing* [2020] BPIR 1069). This distinction between corporate and personal insolvency practice is said to be based upon the dictates of humanity.

Severance of joint tenancies

It is a well-established aspect of land law that a bankruptcy order made against a joint tenant of real property operates so as to sever the joint tenancy and create a tenancy in common in equal shares (*Re Butler's Trusts* [1888] 38 Ch.D 286). This severance is not a disposition that is rendered void.

In the circumstances of a deceased individual who is subsequently subject to an insolvent estate administration order, then changes introduced by s.12(1) Insolvency Act 2000 mitigate the potentially difficult situation of the 'relation back' of the insolvency order to the date of death so as to sever the tenancy and preclude a surviving joint tenant's right of survivorship (eg. *Re Palmer (Gavin)(Deceased)(A Debtor)* [1994] Ch 316. Pursuant to s.421A IA 1986, where:

- An insolvency administration order has been made in relation to the estate of a deceased person, and

- The petition was presented within five-years of the date of death, and

- The deceased was a joint tenant of a property, then

- The court may on the application of the trustee under the insolvent administration order make an order compelling the surviving tenant(s) to pay an amount not exceeding the value lost to the estate by virtue of the survivorship.

CHAPTER THREE

REMEDIES AND DEFENCES

The nature of the remedy

Ss.127 and 284 IA 1986 do not create free-standing causes of action or rights to recovery, but merely void the dispositions in question. The actual right of recovery is under the common law for restitution analogous to an unjust enrichment claim (*Hollicourt (Contracts) Ltd v Bank of Ireland [2001] Ch. 555* for s.127, and *Re Ahmed (A Debtor)* [2018] EWCA Civ 519 for s.284). This is because the payments are 'void' by law, so the recipient does not take title to the goods and has been unjustly enriched at the expense of the insolvent estate.

- When the disposition is of money, then repayment of the same sum plus interest is the usual course of remedy (*Re Officeserve Technologies Ltd (in liq)* [2018] EWHC 2168 (Ch)).

- Likewise, if the disposition is of a physical asset of some kind such as a piece of artwork, then return of the asset is the appropriate remedy, or the monetary value of the asset of it is no longer held by the recipient.

- More difficulties arise if the disposition is of an asset with a fluctuating value such as shares, and such instances will be fact specific. If the value of the shareholding has diminished significantly during the period after which the third-party recipient received it, then the office-holder might seek equitable compensation akin to the price of the shareholding when it would have been sold had it remained in the insolvent estate. In one such instance, the sale period was considered to be three- to six-months after a bankruptcy at the 'fair value' of the shareholding in that period (*Re Ahmed (A Debtor)* [2018] EWCA Civ 519). Alternatively, if the recipient sold the shares a few days after receipt, then the office-holder might seek the value received by the recipient as sale proceeds.

Allied proceedings

A void disposition application pursuant to s.127 IA 1986 does not give rise to a cause of action against the directors of a company, but if loss can be shown then a claim for a misfeasance pursuant to s.212 IA 1986 for breaches of fiduciary duties under the Companies Act 2006 might be brought against the directors in tandem with an application against the recipient of the disposition (eg. *Re Brothers Produce Ltd* [2022] EWHC 291 (Ch)). S.212 IA 1986 is not a freestanding cause of action, but a procedural gateway for bringing fiduciary duty claims, and any such claim will need to plead the breach of duty. Such an approach can be useful where there is a risk that the recipient will not be able to make restitution for the void disposition because of limited assets.

Similarly, the making of void dispositions might form part of the foundation for a disqualification order under the Company Director Disqualification Act 1986, although it would likely need to be made in relation to dispositions for the personal benefit of the director and/or in conjunction with other impugned behaviour (*Re St John Law Ltd* [2019] EWHC 459 (Ch)). Such disqualification orders can be coupled with compensation orders that require the director to make payment to the company (*Re Noble Vinters Ltd* [2019] EWHC 2806 (Ch)), although such relief cannot be sought by the liquidator themselves but rather the Secretary of State.

Effect of void disposition on reviewable transaction claims for unlawful preferences or transactions at an undervalue

One of the most powerful weapons for office-holders in liquidations and bankruptcies is the ability to reopen transactions entered into for a number of years prior to the onset of insolvency of an individual, and reclaim sums that were either paid in preference to one individual creditor over the general body of creditors under ss.239 (corporate) and 340 (personal) IA 1986, or transactions at an undervalue under ss.238 (corporate) and 339 (personal) IA 1986. These provisions do not overlap with void dispositions.

In the context of corporate insolvency:

- Where a liquidation is preceded by an administration, then the 'relevant time' ends with the appointment of the administrator (for appointments by way of qualified floating charge holder), the date of the making of an administration order, or the notice by directors of an intention to appoint an administrator (s.240(3)(d) IA 1986).

- The power of liquidators to use ss.239 and 240 IA 1986 includes the 'relevant period' up to the 'commencement of winding-up,' which will be presentation of the winding-up petition (s.240(3)(e) IA 1986).

In the context of personal bankruptcy:

- The 'relevant time' is defined as being the period ending with the making of the bankruptcy application or presentation of the bankruptcy petition (s.341(1)(a) IA 1986).

S.423 IA 1986 governs transactions defrauding creditors, which is an amended form of a transaction at an undervalue claim which has no 'relevant time,' and can reach back in time within out limit. As there is no definition for 'relevant time,' there is no easy statutory answer as to whether it can overlap with void dispositions, but it is suggested that similar rules will follow as relate to preferences and transactions at an undervalue, above.

The position of a secured creditor

A secured creditor with a floating charge over the assets which formed the basis of a void disposition will have their charge attach to the receipts of any void disposition claim as title never left the company due to the transaction having been avoided as a matter of statute (*Mond v Hammond Suddards* [2000] Ch 40).

Defences

Basic defences

Baring the issuing of a validation order application either before or after the office-holder issues a void disposition claim, then the defences available to the recipient of a void disposition are relatively limited.

- The starting point for any defence is to consider the constituent elements of the impugned disposition: when was it made, to whom was it made, and was the company the beneficial owner of the asset.

- In most cases, those elements will have already been investigated by the office-holder and addressed in the supporting witness statement to the issued application, but there might be arguments to raise as to the recipient receiving the monies as a ministerial agent on behalf of another recipient and thereby not taking beneficial ownership of the disposition (eg. *Prest v Petrodel Resources Ltd* [2013] UKSC 34 for an example of ministerial receipt).

- Likewise, an office-holder might not have the complete picture of any trust structure underpinning the asset disposed, whereas the recipient might. If the recipient can point to the company having no beneficial interest in an asset disposed, then there is no unjust enrichment at the expense of the company.

- Similarly, if the company is the beneficial owner of an asset held on trust by another party as trustee, who disposes of it in a situation similar to that explored above in *Akers v Samba Financial Group* [2017] UKSC 6, then the company might not have a claim.

- In personal bankruptcy, the statutory defence in favour of equity's darling in s.284(4) IA 1986 is available, and this is addressed in detail, below. This defence is not available in corporate insolvency save for situations such as *Akers v Samba,* above.

- Limitation is always a procedural defence, and is explored below.

- There has been much judicial ink spilled regarding the potential for a change of position defence, which I consider in greater detail below.

- Insolvency set-off might operate so as to extinguish the remedy.

Limitation Issues

Recent case law has determined that the appropriate limitation period for claims arising from void dispositions is governed by s.9 Limitation Act 1980, and is six-years from the date of the winding-up order rather than from the payment (*Re Changtel Solutions UK Ltd* [2022] EWHC 694 (Ch)). A similar reasoning would apply to a bankruptcy void disposition claim arising from s.284 IA 1986.

If an office-holder is issuing an application based upon a void disposition, then they must ensure that the application is issued prior to expiration of the limitation deadline.

- While there is allowance for supporting evidence to be filed later (see below, Chapter Five on procedure), it is best practice to file a witness statement at the same time.

- There is a practice that sometimes appears whereby an office-holder issues a bare application with little supporting evidence, and then files a witness statement much later asserting facts or issues that did not otherwise appear on the face of the application notice. This can lead to significant issues upon later applications to amend an application to give better particulars whereby the Court might refuse to have regard to the matters included in the statement (*Re CL Realisations Ltd (in liq.)* [2025] EWHC 796 (Ch)).

- To avoid any arguments that a later service of a witness statement cannot be relied upon as putting facts in issue for the purpose of amendments, it is best practice to either include a fully settled witness statement at the time of issue, or identify the subsequent statement with specifics and file as soon as possible and with alacrity.

Is change of position a defence?

A change of position defence is a common law defence found in claims based upon unjust enrichment and restitution (eg. *Lipkin Gorman (A Firm) v Karpnale Ltd* [1991] 2 AC 548). In summary, a change of position defence exists where the recipient of funds that might otherwise form the basis of an unjust enrichment claim has changed their position in such a way that it would be inequitable to compel repayment. An example might be where an individual received monies in good faith and proceeded to spend those funds on a purchase that they otherwise might not have done believing they were entitled to use of the monies; such as payment for a private medical treatment they might not otherwise have been able to afford. There are various exceptions to this defence which preclude its use:

- A change of position cannot be founded upon normal outgoings such as living expenses or mortgage expenses – the receipt of the funds must have caused the recipient to change their position to do something out of the ordinary.

- Spending received funds after knowledge of the facts giving rise to the subsequent impugning of the payment will undercut a change of position such as knowing of an outstanding petition or receiving a letter before claim.

- If the payment was converted into an existing asset, then it might be argued there is no change of position where repayment is inequitable, such as the use of received funds to pay down mortgage principle sums, so as to swell the recipient's existing assets.

The potential for change of position to be a defence in void dispositions cases has been raised as a possibility in this century (*Rose v AIB Group (UK) Plc* [2003]), and more recent case law has confirmed that such a defence does exist as a possibility (*Re Fowlds* [2021] EWHC 2149 (Ch) in the context of antecedent transaction claims). However, such a defence must be balanced against the underlying policy of insolvency law and the *pari passu* principle, and it must be considered through the same test as a validation order, as set out below (*Re Changtel Solutions UK Ltd* [2022] EWHC 694 (Ch)).

While the change of position defence is available, it is highly unlikely to succeed on its own, and it is suggested a party considering such a defence should seek a validation order, if possible.

Insolvency Set-off

Insolvency set-off is a statutory creature that exists to provide an automatic set-off between debts existing at the date of the insolvency order between two parties that arise from mutual dealings. In corporate insolvency it is found at r14.25 IR 2016, and in bankruptcy at s.323 IA 1986. The set-off does not extinguish a cause of action, but requires an account to be taken of all sums due back and forth between the parties.

- The corporate insolvency set-off in r14.25 IR 2016 is said to concern mutual debts 'before the company goes into liquidation,' which is not defined, but the context of the rule would seem to suggest that the date for determining the set-off is the actual making of the order. Sub-rule r14.25(6) defines 'mutual dealing' as excluding any debts that arise where the non-insolvent party has notice of the petition, which would suggest that debts incurred in the 'relevant period' between petition and winding-up order would still operate as part of the set-off and so would liabilities arising from void dispositions.

- The personal bankruptcy set-off in s.323 IA 1986 is said to operate as of the 'commencement of the bankruptcy,' which immediately harkens in the mind of an insolvency practitioner to presentation of the petition, but it should be remembered that 'commencement of insolvency' is a term used for corporate insolvency and not bankruptcy. Further, s.323(3) IA 1986 makes reference to sums due from the bankrupt to a third-party where that party has notice of the petition falling outside of the set-off, so presumably as with corporate winding-up liability void dispositions would be included in the set-off.

The effect of the set-off is such that where a third-party is owed sums by the bankrupt, and owes monies to the bankrupt, then those sums will be set off £1 for £1. This is an exception to the ratable distribution system of the *pari passu* system.

Equity's darling and the special defence in personal bankruptcy under s.284(4)

Personal bankruptcy contains the specific defence of s.284(4) IA 1986 that is not otherwise found in corporate insolvency:

> *(4) The preceding provisions of this section do not give a remedy against any person—*
>
> > *(a) in respect of any property or payment which he received before the commencement of the bankruptcy in good faith, for value and without notice that the bankruptcy application had been made or (as the case may be) that the bankruptcy petition had been presented, or*

> *(b) in respect of any interest in property which derives from an interest in respect of which there is, by virtue of this subsection, no remedy.*

The defence embodied within s.284(4)(a) IA 1986 is akin to the old equitable defence of 'equity's darling,' which most lawyers are taught in the context of property law, and which protects a bone fide purchaser for value without prior notice of an equitable interest in the property.

The defence has a number of sub-elements which must all be established to rely on the sub-section and defeat a claim pursuant to s.284 IA 1986:

- '*Good Faith*:' the term 'good faith' connotates more than mere personal honesty and the absence of dishonesty, so that a recipient who knew of the constituent elements of the potential bankruptcy (such as financial distress of the bankrupt) but buries their head in the sand to avoid learning of any petition or risk thereof would not be acting in good faith (*Sands v Wright* [2010] 2174 (Ch)).

- '*Value*:' the term value does not require full value to be given by the recipient, and thus they might have received the disposition at an undervalue from the perspective of the bankrupt (*Re Wasu* [2021] EWHC 96 (Ch)), which does raise the spectre of a loophole within the insolvency regime whereby a transaction at an undervalue could exist post-petition. Likewise, it is unnecessary for the value to have been given directly to the bankrupt (*Re Wasu* [2021] EWHC 96 (Ch), applying by analogy the reasoning in *Akers v Samba Financial Group* [2017] UKSC 6).

- '*Without notice*:' this term is defined within the words of the sub-section. The recipient having knowledge of the petition having been presented will render this defence unavailable.

As noted above in relation to the definition of '*value*,' the existence of s.284(4) IA 1986 as a defence creates a potential loophole whereby post-petition transactions at an undervalue or preferences which would otherwise be attackable under ss.339 and 340 IA 1986 but for the petition having been presented have a defence not otherwise available. In the 19th Century an attempt was made to mitigate this loophole by arguing that a void disposition that amounted to a preference was a fraud conducted by the bankrupt and thereby not bound by the protections of then available statutory defence (*Re Badham* [1893] 10 Mor. 252 and s.49 Bankruptcy Act 1883), but this was subsequently not followed and highly unlikely to be available to any present office-holders (*Re Seymour* [1937] Ch 668 ChD).

The further defence in s.284(4)(b) IA 1986 protects the interest of a third-party who receives the property in question from the original recipient of the bankrupt. In essence, it extends the defence to a third-party not expressly covered by sub-section (a) as the original recipient.

As a final point, the hypothetical defence to a restitution claim of '*passing on*' is not available as a matter of English and Welsh law (*Croxen & Others v Gas and Electricity markets Authority & Others* [2022] EWHC 2826 (Ch)).

CHAPTER FOUR

VALIDATION ORDERS

What is a validation order?

Validation applications are regular parasites attached to winding-up and bankruptcy petitions and any subsequent compulsory insolvency orders. They are based upon the elastic terms '*unless the court orders otherwise*' in s.127(1) IA 1986 and '*except to the extent that it is or was made with the consent of the court, or is or was subsequently ratified by the court*' in s.284(1) IA 1986, which give the court the power to 'validate' a transaction so that it is not avoided. The court can exercise this power prospectively or retrospectively, and before or after the making of any compulsory insolvency order. The primary question the court will ask is whether the transaction in question is for the benefit, or potential benefit, of the body of creditors as a whole, or at least whether it will not prejudice the body of creditors.

Standing to apply and the parties to the application

In the period between the presentation of a petition and the making of a compulsory insolvency order (if one is made), then either the debtor or the third-party recipient of a disposition may make a validation order application. Validation order applications are concerned with the solvency of the debtor and the potential effect on the general body of creditors, so the reality of any application by a third-party recipient is that it will need to be made with some cooperation from the debtor so that the relevant financial information can be obtained. As discussed below, unless the applicant can satisfy the court as to the various solvency issues, then a validation order will not be granted.

After a winding-up or bankruptcy order has been made, then the validation order can be sought retrospectively by the third-party recipient, and will typically be brought as a form of a defence against a mooted or issued void disposition claim.

Timing

Validation orders can be sought prospectively and retrospectively, and can be sought either before the compulsory insolvency order or after it is made, but the court's approach to applications depends on when the application is heard and the circumstances in which it is heard (as set out below). Obviously, an application made after an insolvency order changes the dynamic of any application as the insolvency of the debtor is a certainty, and the test to be met by the third-party recipient becomes more difficult. In practice, if a potential recipient is aware of pending insolvency proceedings, then they should seek – or require the debtor to seek – a validation order prospectively before the disposition is made so as to avoid any problems of void dispositions down the road.

Pre-insolvency validation order

Validation order applications made before a compulsory insolvency order are 'easier' than those made after as there is more scope to argue that a debtor may be solvent. This question is settled as a matter of fact after a court makes a winding-up or bankruptcy order.

What is the General Test

As noted in the introduction to this text, the fundamental rule of insolvency law that the interest of the body of creditors as a whole is paramount to that of any individual creditor is the guiding principle for validation orders – whether prospective, retrospective, or sought after the insolvency order.

- This fundamental principle is the guiding authority for validation orders such that the applicants must demonstrate the special circumstances exist which make a particular transaction either for the benefit of the body of creditors as a whole, or at least not prejudicial to any other creditors (*Express Electrical Distributors Ltd v Beavis* [2016] EWCA Civ 765).

- This general rule is embodied in the PDIP at paragraph 9.11.7, which requires for any validation order that:

  > *"The Court will need to be satisfied by credible evidence either that the company is solvent and able to pay its debts as they fall due or that a particular transaction or series of transactions in respect of which the order is sought will be beneficial to or will not prejudice the interests of all the unsecured creditors as a class."*

- Solvency can be a tricky question. In the corporate sphere, a company can be insolvent on either the balance-sheet or the cash-flow test (s.123 IA 1986). Balance-sheet insolvency is the comparison of the overall debt and asset position of a company, and must take into consideration the present assets against present and future liabilities (*BNY Corporate Trustee Services Limited v Eurosail-UK* [2013] UKSC 28). Cash-flow insolvency is a much easier test – has a company failed, or will it be unable in the immediate future, to pay a particular debt because it does not have the present resources to do so. Personal bankruptcy is concerned with the cash-flow test (whether a statutory demand has been paid or not). In either event, those seeking a validation order will need to demonstrate that the debtor is solvent, or the transaction will benefit all creditors. This can require detailed consideration and disclosure of the debtor's financial records, and for this reason the debtor company or individual must be involved in the application (if prior to any insolvency order).

- Generally speaking, the Court will prospectively grant a validation order where there is no risk to other creditors (such as payment in full value for a post-petition transaction that allows for continued trading of a company) or that the transaction will improve the position of the debtor (*RC Brewery Ltd v HMRC* [2013] EWHC 1184 (Ch). Where the payment is an existing debt so that on first glance it appears the individual creditor is being preferred over other creditors, then the applicant will need to satisfy the court that such a payment is essential for some reason. This can take the form of a payment for trading supplies or stock which will allow the debtor to potentially trade their way out of insolvency or at least improve their financial position in respect to any subsequent insolvency (*Re Gray's Inn Construction Co Ltd* [1980] 1 WLR 711).

- A potential example might be a final payment to contractors to finish the construction of a building that can then be marketed and sold at a higher value then the unfinished property would have in any insolvency. Another classic example is the payment of older invoices for fuel oil supplied to a haulage company where payment of old debts was required before future fuel oil would be supplied allowing the company to continue its trade (and therefore profit for the benefit of creditors generally) (*Denney v John Hudson & Co ltd* [1992] BCC 503).

- Transactions at an undervalue to the debtor are unlikely to be validated as such a transaction would normally be of prejudice to the general body of creditors, and if seeking a prospective validation order then evidence of the full value of the consideration to the debtor should be provided with the validation application evidence (PDIP 9.11.6).

- In the context of corporate validation orders, older case-law suggested that transactions made in 'good faith' without notice of a petition were more likely to be validated applying a test akin to the statutory defence in s.284(6) IA 1986 for personal bankruptcy, but this old view has largely been swept away by recent case-law which holds that no such exception applies under s.127 IA 1986 (*Officeserve Technologies Ltd (in liq)* [2018] EWHC 2168 (Ch)). Rather, an applicant should focus their attention on the issue of benefit to the body of creditors as a whole.

- Conversely, in personal bankruptcy, if an applicant can meet the test of good faith receipt without notice for full value (matching the defence in s.284(6) IA 1986), then the validation order will likely be granted.

<u>Validation after the winding-up or bankruptcy order</u>

Validation orders sought after a winding-up or bankruptcy order are more 'difficult' in that the insolvency of the debtor has been established as a matter of fact, and the potential arguments as to solvency fall away.

- In such circumstances the court will be most interested in whether the particular transaction benefitted the greater body of creditors as a whole. An applicant will need to demonstrate how the payment benefitted all of the creditors, which might be possible if it gave rise to an ability to trade for longer at a profit, or where the consideration flowing back to the insolvent somehow gave rise to a subsequent profit or acquisition of an asset that can be realised in the insolvency.

Specific instances

Payments of a winding-up or bankruptcy petition debt

As discussed above, there is a risk on every petitioner that where a debtor pays a settlement of a petition debt from their own funds a different creditor might substitute into the petition and achieve a subsequent insolvency order that voids the settlement payment. To avoid this eventuality, and if third-party funds are not available to pay a settlement, then a validation order should be sought prospectively. This should be sought by the debtor and the creditor, and it will need to be justified according the tests set out above. A petitioning creditor who chooses not to seek a validation order for such a payment, or closes their eyes to the potential of other creditors, might have a painful lesson in void dispositions at a later date.

Legal fees

As noted above, legal fees are not excepted from the ambit of void dispositions, and legal advisors will need to ensure that they are either paid by third-parties, or that fees paid to them by a debtor facing a petition have been validated. There is no certainty of such validation.

- Within the sphere of personal insolvency, there is a greater likelihood of a court validating legal fees (as well as reasonable living expenses) for a debtor due to the dictates of humanity (*Andrew v Kingsway Asset Leasing [2020] B.P.I.R. 1069*), but an applicant applying for a validation order in respect to legal fees will still need to make a good disclosure of their financial position or the application will be dismissed as they have no automatic right to a validation order (*Rio Properties Inc v Al-Midani* [2003] BPIR 128).

- A validation order in respect to legal fees for proceedings other than the petition will need to demonstrate what value will accrue to the general body of creditors, and will need to properly explain in evidence a breakdown of the fees. Failure to do either of these will likely result in dismissal of the application (*State Bank of India v Mallya [2021] EWHC 1740 (Ch)*

- Conversely, an attempt to validate legal fees in respect to a petition where the purpose is merely to delay the making of an order rather than a good faith attempt to defend against it will not be validated (*Re Brewery Ltd v HMRC* [2013] EWHC 1184 (Ch) where the company sought to restrain advertisement of the petition but did not subsequently object to the petition itself)

CHAPTER FIVE

PROCEDURAL MATTERS

Procedure is the life blood of legal practitioners, and one of the more daunting and complex elements of claims for those who are not legally qualified. What is set out below is a general overview of the procedure for making and defending void disposition claims, and making validation order applications including where they are to be made, what they should comprise, and what route will be followed.

This book is not the place for an exhaustive review of the courts of England and Wales, but in general the courts which might have jurisdiction to hearing the relevant applications are:

- The Couty Court, which is now deemed to be one national court with individual sittings in specific locales (eg. the County Court at Romford), and which is the likely venue for smaller value matters. The County Court at Central London has a number of specialist business and property judges with particular expertise in insolvency matters, and they often hear contentious matters that have been issued in Central London or in other London County Court locations that have been transferred.

- The specialist Insolvency and Companies Court in the High Court in London where six specialist Insolvency and Companies Court Judges sit daily along with various deputies. For any claim or validation application starting in London these judges will case-manage the matter, and will likely retain jurisdiction to a final hearing. In some instances where the value or complexity is of a particular level it might be moved up to a High Court judge. Conversely, the High Court has the power to transfer matters, and if it is of a sufficiently low value or complexity it might be transferred to the County Court at Central London and its specialist insolvency judges. There is an analogous level of judges known as 'Masters' who sit on chancery matters and in the King's Bench, and who sometimes might deal with insolvency related matters.

- In district registries of the High Court outside of London there are often specialist district judges who fulfil a similar role to the ICC Judges in London (eg. the District Court in Birmingham). Claims and applications might be first heard by district judges in these instances for directions, and then dealt with on a final basis by those district judges or 'moved up' to a High Court judge.

- Routes of appeal between levels of court are set out in greater detail below.

Regardless of where an insolvency application is issued, it is deemed to be allocated to the multi-track so that Part 29 of the CPR applies.

Depending on the court in question, only certain individuals may make submissions to the court.

- Solicitors and chartered legal executive advocates have rights of audience in the County Court and can appear before judges in the Insolvency and Companies Court and masters.

- Only barristers, or advocates who have obtained higher rights of audience, can appear before a High Court judge or above.

- Litigants in person can appear on their own behalf in every court, and can be assisted by a McKenzie Friend, but cannot be represented by another individual unless they are legally qualified with appropriate rights of audience such as a barrister or solicitor advocate or chartered legal executive advocate. A McKenzie Friend can assist a litigant in person, but cannot speak on their behalf in court. In practice, where a litigant in person has a poor grasp of English, or is disabled in such a fashion that they cannot speak on their own behalf, then a judge might be willing to allow a McKenzie Friend to speak on the behalf of the litigant.

- Litigants in person should be aware that there is no special treatment for litigants in person under the CPR, and they will be expected to conform to the same rules as all other litigants (*Barton v Wright Hassall LLP* [2018] UKSC 12).

The Court

Void disposition claims and validation applications will by their nature only follow the presentation of a winding-up or bankruptcy petition, and potentially a final order. As a result, proceedings will have been issued already in a particular court by the issuing of the petition and/or the making of the final order, and this will govern where any subsequent application can be made. A 'claim number' will be assigned to the petition, and any subsequent applications should be made in reference to this number.

In insolvency, claims for void dispositions or applications for validation orders should be made to the court in which the petition was issued and/or the final insolvency order made. As an example, if a petition is issued in the Insolvency and Companies Court in London, then any application for a validation order or a subsequent void disposition claim should be issued in that court unless the matter has been transferred elsewhere.

Proceedings on insolvency matters are public hearings, and members of the public are entitled to observe. In the High Court, it is not uncommon for a court reporter to be circulating and requesting copies of skeleton arguments from the various advocates of a case. Litigants should be made aware that if the case is one of high public interest involving a celebrity or of particular details that might interest the public at large, then there is a possibility that a summary of the matter will make its way into public newspapers.

The different types of judges (including modes of address)

For those who do not appear in court regularly, or for litigants in person, the modes of address for different judges can be a stressful distraction.

- In the County Court the level of judges are district judges and circuit judges (or recorders). District judges are likely to deal with most matters, and should be referred to as '*Judge.*' Circuit judges (or recorders) will typically deal with more complex matters in the Couty Court, and should be referred to as '*Your Honour.*'

- Insolvency and Company Court Judges should be referred to as '*Judge.*' Likewise, a Master of chancery or in the King's Bench Division should be referred to as '*Judge.*'

- High Court, Court of Appeal, Privy Council, and Supreme Court judges should be referred to as '*My Lord / Your Lordship.*'

As an allied point to modes of address, court dress for advocates differs depending on the level of the judge.

- Unless the judge otherwise requires it, appearances before District Judges to High Court judges on validation orders will only require standard court dress of suits.

- Where a trial of a void disposition claim might involve witness handling, then there is a strong possibility robes and wigs will be required, and the advocate should have their clerk check with the judge's clerk as to whether robing will be required.

- For appeals to the High Court and Court of Appeal, then the expectation is that the advocates should be robed and wigged.

- For appeals to the Supreme Court, then the expectation is that only business suits are necessary, and robes and wigs should not be worn.

- Litigants in person are obviously not required to wear particular court dress, but as a matter of basic logic they are encouraged to wear smart clothes.

The Application

Insolvency matters sit outside the normal rules of commencing proceedings in the CPR, and both void disposition 'claims' and validation order applications are commenced by way of an insolvency application, which consists of a short application notice and accompanying witness statement. This procedure is streamlined and cheap in comparison to Part 7 and 8 proceedings under the CPR, and reflects the natural state of insolvency when the paramount concern should be the preservation of assets for the creditors by keeping fees and expenses as low as possible.

There is no standard form for an insolvency application (as compared to a claim form for Part 7 or a N244 application form under the CPR), and it merely has to comply with the requirements of contents set out in r1.35 2016 Rules.

- A standard template example can be found on the gov.uk website as well as guidance notes for completing the document.

- The application notice should contain details of the relief sought, for example:

  - '*A declaration that a payment of £1 on 1 January 2025 is void pursuant to s.127 1986* Act.'

  - '*That the Respondent do pay the sum of £1 to the Applicant.*'

- The fee for issuing an insolvency application is only £112, which is significantly lower than those found in Part 7 proceedings. This is especially useful for office-holders where the insolvent estate has limited (or no) funds. In practice, office-holders will sometimes issue a number of void disposition claims against multiple third-party recipients on one application notice to save fees, with the result that all matters will be case-managed together on an initial basis. Some courts may take issue with this approach.

- A draft order should always be included with the application when issued, and any advocate appearing at a subsequent hearing should include a copy of a draft order annexed to their skeleton. It is often the case that the contents of the draft order will change depending on what occurs during the prosecution of an application, so an advocate is advised to consider their draft order in advance of any hearing and adjust the recitals, declarations, and orders to match the current state of play.

- In the High Court, both in London and the district registries, applications are issued using the CE-File electronic filing system, which must be used by legally represented parties. Individuals appearing in person can apply with paper copies of applications. All documents subsequently required to be 'filed' in the proceedings will need to be filed on the CE-File.

The Parties

A void disposition claim can be brought by the office-holder of the insolvency, either the liquidator or the trustee in bankruptcy, and the respondent to such a claim will be the recipient of the disposition.

The parties to the validation order will depend on when the application is being made.

- Post-insolvency order, the validation order applicant will be the recipient of the void disposition, and the respondent will be the office-holder on behalf of the insolvent.

- Pre-insolvency order, the applicant(s) will be the insolvent and potential recipient, and the respondent will be the petitioner.

Recent years have seen the rise of specific litigation funding companies purchasing claims that would normally be vested in an office-holder such as breach of fiduciary duty claims, or debt claims.

- In such circumstances, the party issuing the claim is not an office-holder, but the assignee of the office-holder. An unanswered question is whether a void disposition claim under ss.127 or 284 IA 1986 can be assigned to a third-party such as a litigation funder.

- Traditionally, it had been held that a liquidator cannot assign a claim for a void disposition under s.127 IA 1986 (*Re Ayala Holdings Ltd (no2)* [1996] 1 BCLC 467), but there is some criticism of this position and it remains open under the amendments to the IA 1986 since *Ayala* as to whether an assignment could be valid.

The evidence in support

The typical insolvency application will not require any traditional pleadings as in Part 7 CPR proceedings, and rather a witness statement will accompany the application notice, which will set out the nature of the application, the relief sought, and the facts giving rise to the relief. It will exhibit all relevant documentation, which should be included with the statement when it is filed and served on any other parties.

- In complex matters, the Court may order points of claim and points of defence to be prepared, which are analogous to traditional Part 7 pleadings, but for void disposition claims this is unlikely unless they are either complex or coupled with other claims.

- An applicant wishing to rely on witness evidence at a hearing must file and serve it no later than 14-business days before a hearing (r12.28 IR 2016), and a respondent no later than five-business days before a hearing. It is not typically required for a respondent to file evidence before the first directions hearing of an application as directions will be given at that time for the filing of evidence (assuming the respondent appears).

- Witness statements should comply with Part 32 of the CPR, but the requirements of CPR practice direction 57AC for the Business and Property Courts do not apply to insolvency proceedings. Witnesses should avoid opining about matters beyond statements of fact, although the nature of using witness statements as pseudo-pleadings requires some linguistic breach of this rule as the various tests for validation orders or void dispositions must be addressed in the statement.

- Office-holders filing a witness statement in support of a void disposition claim should include as an exhibit to the statement all relevant material regarding the claim, and anything they think might be relevant for the respondent. Where they are filing evidence in response to a retrospective validation order, then this might involve the exhibiting of relevant financial information of the insolvent so that the solvency issues can be properly reviewed, and especially as they are likely the only party in possession of such material.

- As noted above, there is a practice amongst some to file an application notice without supporting evidence when a limitation period is about to expire. The issuing of an application is necessary in such circumstances to avoid a limitation defence, and often the party will then seek to amend their case subsequently to improve it with more legal consideration. A statement will then be filed a few months after the application is issued but before the initial hearing, and after the limitation period has expired. This 'protective' approach should be avoided, if possible, as a statement filed post-limitation deadline and separate from the application notice will not be available as a tool for claiming facts were already 'in issue' for any subsequent amendment application (*Re CL Realisations 2020 Ltd (in liq)* [2025] EWHC 796 (Ch)).

It is better for all matters in issue to be raised in a statement accompanying the application notice.

Service

As a general matter, service of applications will follow rules similar to the CPR. Application notices in insolvency proceedings are generally treated as analogous to claim forms, and service must be made on other parties by no later than 14-days before the first hearing.

- Service will be deemed to have occurred as provided for in the CPR r6.14. Typically, this is the second business day after the mode of service has been accomplished. Where possible, it is useful for parties to agree that service can be done by electronic means, ie. email.

- Where a respondent to an application or claim is outside of the jurisdiction, which might be the case in void disposition claim, an application will need to be made for permission to service out of the jurisdiction according to Part 6 of the CPR and Practice Direction 6B. This will need to set out what ground for permission out is relied upon in paragraph 3.1 Practice Direction 6B, that the applicant believes there is a reasonable prospect of success, and the address of the respondent.

Hearings

Void disposition claims and validation order applications will invariably be heard in court, and will not be dealt with on the papers unless the parties have agreed a consent order. By way of general notes:

- In the High Court, and following conclusion of any hearing, the court will ask the advocates to agree the form of order to be sealed by the court. If an advocate has prepared and annexed a copy of a draft order to their skeleton, then the judge might comment on it and suggest any changes that are necessary, which greatly simplifies the task of composing and agreeing the order. In other circumstances, the advocates might need to correspond at length on an appropriate agreed wording of the order, which can lead to follow-on disputes.

- Where the litigants are all in person with no qualified legal professional appearing, then the court will maintain carriage of the order and will draft and serve the sealed order on the litigants.

- For all hearings a bundle should be prepared by the applicant party. Most courts operate a policy that if a hearing bundle is not provided by a party, then the matter will be adjourned to a further hearing in the future (or dismissed in extreme instances where similar issues has arisen previously). Where the applicant is not legally represented but the respondent is, then the respondent's solicitors should either correspond with the applicant to arrange for an agreed bundle to be filed or should take carriage of the bundle themselves. The contents of hearing bundles should comply with those set out in the Chancery Guide, which can be found online. Courts typically deprecate parties filing duelling bundles that only include their own relevant material, and every opportunity should be taken to agree a reasonable bundle wherein only relevant documents are included in the bundle.

- A .pdf of the hearing bundle should be filed on CE-File in addition to a hard copy of the bundle being filed at court. If a matter is only being heard virtually, then the court might give directions that only .pdf virtual bundles are necessary, but litigants should be aware that some judges request hard copy bundles in any event.

Initial hearing(s)

Any insolvency application seeking substantive relief will be listed for an initial directions hearing of approximately 15-minutes, and which will be listed subject to the current availability of the court where the application is issued.

- In some courts there might be a delay of a few months before a directions hearing is listed, while in others it may be a much shorter period.

- The recent experience has been that matters issued in London, either the Insolvency and Companies Court or the County Court at Central London, take longer to be heard than those in district registries of the High Court, such as Leeds, due to the number of applications being issued in London.

- Initial hearings will sometimes be heard virtually. In the Insolvency and Companies Court in London the initial hearings are currently being heard by way of Microsoft Teams, although in-person hearings can be accommodated if the virtual option is not appropriate for a particular litigant. The practice in other courts varies, and in the County Court at Central London initial directions hearings are often in person.

- If a legal representative is appearing at the hearing, then they should file a skeleton argument. In light of the increasing demands on court staff, a skeleton argument should be filed at least 24-hours before the hearing, but no later than 4pm the day before the hearing as the judge will not have an opportunity to read it otherwise.

The purpose of the initial hearing is to set directions for final determination of a matter.

- In the case of both void disposition claims and validation order applications this will typically consist of a right to the respondent to file evidence in response, and a corresponding right to the applicant to file evidence in reply. Typically, the evidence in response will be ordered to be filed around 28-days after the hearing, and the evidence in reply between 14- and 21-days after that. However, the judge has a discretion on such matters, and can order longer or shorter periods depending on the particular circumstances of the matter and the parties' submissions. For instance, where a direction hearing is heard in early December, then the judge will often give a longer time for evidence in response as the intervening holiday period will mean that legal representatives are unavailable. For prospective validation orders, then the time frame is likely to be condensed due to the nature of the payment needing to be made.

- In insolvency proceedings, issues of disclosure are dealt with by exhibiting all relevant documents to the witness statements. As such, there is rarely a need for orders as to disclosure. In some instances, a respondent facing an application from an office-holder will request the right to review the documents in the possession of the office-holder as relevant accounting and financial information as the solvency of the insolvent will be included therein, and the respondent is unlikely to be able to address the financial position otherwise. However, as set out above, the office-holder should include all relevant financial information in any application they bring for a void disposition, or in any evidence in response to a post-insolvency retrospective validation order.

- Cost budgeting is excluded from insolvency proceedings unless otherwise ordered, and it will rarely appear in a void disposition claim unless it is coupled with other proceedings such as a complex misfeasance claim where the parties desire cost budgeting.

- As set out above, witness statements in insolvency proceedings are not included in the general CPR rules as to statements. This is a common-sense position where office-holders have no personal knowledge of the actions of an insolvent, and can merely present documentary evidence and its conclusions.

- Provision should be included in the directions order for filing of skeletons and a joint authorities bundle, which should typically be filed a few days before the final hearing / trial of the matter so that all parties have a chance to consider the arguments and refine them in oral submissions to the court. Likewise, provision should be included for filing a final trial bundle, and as noted above, if only one party is legally represented then that party should seek to take carriage of the bundle to ensure it is properly prepared.

- The parties should provide a realistic time estimate for the final hearing / trial, and in practice will not need to extend beyond one-day. However, where matters are complex or part of proceedings involving multiple causes of action, and where live evidence will be necessary, then time estimates are likely to be longer.

For both void disposition claims and validation orders, a final order can be made at the initial hearing if there is no appearance by a respondent to contest the application. In my experience, where a respondent to a void disposition claim is unable to identify a potential defence to the claim, then the court might be minded to make a final order at the first hearing.

The parties often agree directions by way of consent order prior to the initial hearing so as to avoid the legal costs of instructing counsel to appear at the hearing. When both sides are legally represented, then this can be a useful and cost effective way of streamlining proceedings.

Final Hearing / Trial

The nature of the final hearing, its time estimate, and whether live evidence will be considered will be determined at the directions hearing.

- For a validation order and a void disposition claim it is unlikely that there will be disputes of fact that require witness handling, but it is a possibility depending on whether particular facts are disputed or not.

- Following the hearing, the judge will either give a decision or will 'reserve' their judgment. In the case of reserved judgments, the judge will consider what judgment to make, and will often deliver judgment in written format some time after the day of the hearing. This may take a few weeks or months depending on the nature and complexity of the matter. Reserved judgments will often be disseminated by the court in draft format a short time prior to being formally 'handed down,' and the contents of these draft judgments cannot be told to anyone other than the litigants involved and their legal team. A breach of this prohibition is a contempt of court and can land a person in jail depending on the circumstances of the breach.

- In urgent matters such as some validation orders, then the judge is more likely to give a decision on the day or very quickly thereafter as the matter is time sensitive.

Urgent hearings

The Insolvency and Companies Court in London operates an urgent applications list a few days per week, in which 'urgent' applications that are time sensitive will be triaged and heard by an ICC Judge.

- Parties seeking to have their applications heard in the urgent list will need to justify the urgency and sign a certificate of urgency in support of the listing.

- This list should only be used for truly urgent matters, and validation orders in the period between the petition and the hearing of the petition would likely constitute urgent business if well founded.

- A claim for a void disposition is highly unlikely to be an urgent matter, and should not be sought to be placed into the urgent list. If there is a risk that the recipient of the void disposition might seek to dissipate their assets to avoid a judgment in the void disposition claim, then a freezing or proprietary injunction can be sought separately to restrain any dissipation, and that might form the basis of an urgent application.

Consequential matters and Appeals

Costs

The general rule on costs is that they 'follow the event,' so that the loser pays the winner's costs of any application. The court has ultimately discretion over costs, and in some instances might reverse this rule where the conduct of the parties warrants it, or there has been intervening without prejudice discussion on a resolution such that the 'loser' made an offer of settlement better than what was ultimately achieved by court order. However, generally speaking:

The route of appeals

A litigant who is unsatisfied with a judgment has the right to seek permission to appeal to a higher court, although the nature of that appeal must be to demonstrate that a judge made a mistake in the judgment rather than asking for a re-hearing of the matter *de novo*.

- Permission to appeal should first be sought from the judge who made the decision, although in most cases this is unlikely to succeed as the judge is unlikely to decide that there is a risk that their judgment was wrong. However, in some instances where the law is not clear, or the value or importance of a case is obviously high, then a judge might be more inclined to grant permission.

- A litigant has two attempts to seek permission to the High Court or the Court of Appeal, as the case may be. First, by making a paper application containing the grounds of appeal and a supporting skeleton argument which will be considered 'on the papers' by a judge who will grant or refuse permission to appeal. Second, if permission is refused on the papers then the applicant is permitted to renew their application and make oral submissions on their permission application.

Appeals from decisions of the County Court, the Insolvency and Companies Court (or the analogous level of district judge in district registries) are to a single judge of the High Court (), and must be made in accordance with the provisions of CPR Part 52 and its various practice directions.

Appeals from the High Court are to the Court of Appeal, and are governed by the provisions of CPR Practice Direction 52C.

Appeals from the Court of Appeal are to the Supreme Court, and are governed by the special procedure rules for the Supreme Court.

- Of note, an application for permission to appeal to the Supreme Court *must* be made to the Court of Appeal first, and only if it is rejected can a litigant seek the permission of the Supreme Court itself.

MORE BOOKS BY LAW BRIEF PUBLISHING

‘The Electronic Communications Code: A Practical Guide – Second Edition’ by Kerry Bretherton KC, James Castle, Mark Loveday
‘A Practical Guide to the Independent School Standards – September 2023 Edition’ by Sarah McKimm
'A Practical Guide to Estate Administration and Crypto Assets' by Richard Marshall
‘A Practical Guide to Parental Alienation in Private and Public Law Children Cases’ by Sam King QC & Frankie Shama
‘Contested Heritage – Removing Art from Land and Historic Buildings’ by Richard Harwood QC, Catherine Dobson, David Sawtell
‘The Limits of Separate Legal Personality: When Those Running a Company Can Be Held Personally Liable for Losses Caused to Third Parties Outside of the Company’ by Dr Mike Wilkinson
‘A Practical Guide to Transgender Law’ by Robin Moira White & Nicola Newbegin
‘A Practical Guide to ‘Stranded Spouses’ in Family Law’ by Mani Singh Basi
‘A Practical Guide to Residential Freehold Conveyancing’ by Lorraine Richardson
‘A Practical Guide to Pensions on Divorce for Lawyers’ by Bryan Scant
‘A Practical Guide to Challenging Sham Marriage Allegations in Immigration Law’ by Priya Solanki
‘A Practical Guide to Digital Communications Evidence in Criminal Law’ by Sam Willis
‘A Practical Guide to Legal Rights in Scotland’ by Sarah-Jane Macdonald
‘A Practical Guide to New Build Conveyancing’ by Paul Sams & Rebecca East
‘A Practical Guide to Inherited Wealth on Divorce’ by Hayley Trim
‘A Practical Guide to Practice Direction 12J and Domestic Abuse in Private Law Children Proceedings’ by Rebecca Cross & Malvika Jaganmohan
‘A Practical Guide to Confiscation and Restraint’ by Narita Bahra QC, John Carl Townsend, David Winch
‘A Practical Guide to the Law of Forests in Scotland’ by Philip Buchan
‘A Practical Guide to Health and Medical Cases in Immigration Law’ by Rebecca Chapman & Miranda Butler
‘A Practical Guide to Bad Character Evidence for Criminal Practitioners by Aparna Rao
‘A Practical Guide to Extradition Law post-Brexit’ by Myles Grandison et al
‘A Practical Guide to Hoarding and Mental Health for Housing Lawyers’ by Rachel Coyle

'Stephens on Contractual Indemnities' by Richard Stephens
'A Practical Guide to the EU Succession Regulation' by Richard Frimston
'A Practical Guide to Solicitor and Client Costs – Second Edition' by Robin Dunne
'Constructive Dismissal – Practice Pointers and Principles' by Benjimin Burgher
'A Practical Guide to Religion and Belief Discrimination Claims in the Workplace' by Kashif Ali
'A Practical Guide to the Law of Medical Treatment Decisions' by Ben Troke
'Fundamental Dishonesty and QOCS in Personal Injury Proceedings: Law and Practice' by Jake Rowley
'A Practical Guide to the Law in Relation to School Exclusions' by Charlotte Hadfield & Alice de Coverley
'A Practical Guide to Divorce for the Silver Separators' by Karin Walker
'The Right to be Forgotten – The Law and Practical Issues' by Melissa Stock
'A Practical Guide to Planning Law and Rights of Way in National Parks, the Broads and AONBs' by James Maurici QC, James Neill et al
'A Practical Guide to Election Law' by Tom Tabori
'A Practical Guide to the Law in Relation to Surrogacy' by Andrew Powell
'A Practical Guide to Claims Arising from Fatal Accidents – Second Edition' by James Patience
'A Practical Guide to Asbestos Claims' by Jonathan Owen & Gareth McAloon
'A Practical Guide to Stamp Duty Land Tax in England and Northern Ireland' by Suzanne O'Hara
'A Practical Guide to the Law of Farming Partnerships' by Philip Whitcomb
'A Practical Guide to the Law of Unlawful Eviction and Harassment – Second Edition' by Stephanie Lovegrove
'A Practical Guide to Costs in Personal Injury Claims – Second Edition' by Matthew Hoe
'A Practical Guide to the General Data Protection Regulation (GDPR) – Second Edition' by Keith Markham
'A Practical Guide to Working with Litigants in Person and McKenzie Friends in Family Cases' by Stuart Barlow
'Protecting Unregistered Brands: A Practical Guide to the Law of Passing Off' by Lorna Brazell
'A Practical Guide to Secondary Liability and Joint Enterprise Post-Jogee' by Joanne Cecil & James Mehigan

'A Practical Guide to the Pre-Action RTA Claims Protocol for Personal Injury Lawyers' by Antonia Ford
'A Practical Guide to Neighbour Disputes and the Law' by Alexander Walsh
'A Practical Guide to Coercive Control for Legal Practitioners and Victims' by Rachel Horman
'A Practical Guide to the Law of Driverless Cars – Second Edition'
by Alex Glassbrook, Emma Northey & Scarlett Milligan
'A Practical Guide to TOLATA Claims' by Greg Williams
'A Practical Guide to Elderly Law – Second Edition' by Justin Patten
'A Practical Guide to Responding to Housing Disrepair and Unfitness Claims' by Iain Wightwick
'A Practical Guide to the Law of Bullying and Harassment in the Workplace' by Philip Hyland
'How to Be a Freelance Solicitor: A Practical Guide to the SRA-Regulated Freelance Solicitor Model' by Paul Bennett
'A Practical Guide to Prison Injury Claims' by Malcolm Johnson
'A Practical Guide to Advising Clients at the Police Station' by Colin Stephen McKeown-Beaumont
'A Practical Guide to Antisocial Behaviour Injunctions – Second Edition' by Iain Wightwick
'Practical Mediation: A Guide for Mediators, Advocates, Advisers, Lawyers, and Students in Civil, Commercial, Business, Property, Workplace, and Employment Cases' by Jonathan Dingle with John Sephton
'The Mini-Pupillage Workbook' by David Boyle
'A Practical Guide to Crofting Law' by Brian Inkster
'A Practical Guide to the Law of Domain Names and Cybersquatting' by Andrew Clemson
'A Practical Guide to the Law of Gender Pay Gap Reporting' by Harini Iyengar
'NHS Whistleblowing and the Law' by Joseph England
'Employment Law and the Gig Economy' by Nigel Mackay & Annie Powell
'A Practical Guide to Noise Induced Hearing Loss (NIHL) Claims' by Andrew Mckie, Ian Skeate, Gareth McAloon
'An Introduction to Beauty Negligence Claims – A Practical Guide for the Personal Injury Practitioner' by Greg Almond
'Intercompany Agreements for Transfer Pricing Compliance' by Paul Sutton
'Zen and the Art of Mediation' by Martin Plowman
'A Practical Guide to Adoption for Family Lawyers' by Graham Pegg

www.ingramcontent.com/pod-product-compliance
Ingram Content Group UK Ltd.
Pitfield, Milton Keynes, MK11 3LW, UK
UKHW020151290926
15471UKWH00004B/799

9 781916 69890